HELPING YOURSELF
HELPING OTHERS

Dealing with
CYBERBULLYING

Derek Miller

Cavendish
Square
New York

Published in 2020 by Cavendish Square Publishing, LLC
243 5th Avenue, Suite 136, New York, NY 10016

Copyright © 2020 by Cavendish Square Publishing, LLC

First Edition

Cataloging-in-Publication Data

Names: Miller, Derek.
Title: Dealing with cyberbullying / Derek Miller.
Description: New York : Cavendish Square Publishing, 2020. |
Series: Helping yourself, helping others | Includes glossary and index.
Identifiers: ISBN 9781502646200 (pbk.) | ISBN 9781502646217 (library bound) |
ISBN 9781502646224 (ebook)
Subjects: LCSH: Cyberbullying--Juvenile literature.
Classification: LCC HV6773.15.C92 M555 2020 | DDC 302.34/3--dc23

Editorial Director: David McNamara
Editor: Caitlyn Miller
Copy Editor: Rebecca Rohan
Associate Art Director: Alan Sliwinski
Designer: Ginny Kemmerer
Production Coordinator: Karol Szymczuk
Photo Research: J8 Media

The photographs in this book are used by permission and through the courtesy of:
(Note: cover, p 4, 17, 22, 30, 37, 52, 55, 71, 76, 85, 92, 96; people in photos are models and the images are being used for illustrative purposes only); Cover CatLane/iStockphoto.com; p. 4 Jeffrey Greenberg/UIG/Getty Images; p. 7 Ponsulak/Shutterstock.com; p. 13 Natee Meepian/Shutterstock.com; p. 17 Iryna Tiumentseva/Shutterstock.com; p. 20 Toby Talbot/AP Images, background (and used throughout the book) Mika Besfamilnaya/Shutterstock.com; p. 22 LightField Studios/Shutterstock.com; p. 25 By Zaur Rahimov/Shutterstock.com; p. 30 Tory Zubovich/Shutterstock.com; p. 35 Kpatyhka/Shutterstock.com; p. 37 inLite studio/ Shutterstock.com; p. 38 Tom Gannam/AP Images; p. 44 Jonathan Hayward/The Canadian Press/AP Images; p. 47 Craig Fry/Yuma Sun/AP Images; p. 49 Robin Marchant/Getty Images; p. 52 MachineHeadz/iStock/Getty Images; p. 55 Image Source/Image Source/ Getty Images; p. 62 Tow qu Photography/Moment/Getty Images; p. 64 Lula Wanderwood/Shutterstock.com; p. 67 SergeyAK/ iStockphoto.com; p. 71 Katarzyna Bialasiewicz/iStockphoto.com; p. 72 Jay LaPrete/AP Images; p. 74 Stephen Coburn/Shutterstock. com; p. 76 Manuel Breva Colmeiro/Moment/Getty Images; p. 83 Rufat Bunyadzada/Shutterstock.com; p. 85 Pixelheadphoto Digitalskillet/Shutterstock.com; p. 88 Pixinoo/Shutterstock.com; p. 92 Africa Studio/Shutterstock.com; p. 95 Annette Birschel/ Picture Alliance/Getty Images; p. 96 Martin-dm/iStockphoto.com.

Printed in the United States of America

Some of the images in this book illustrate individuals who are models. The depictions do not imply actual situations or events.

CONTENTS

Chapter 1

The Facts About Cyberbullying

The internet and smartphones have made it easier than ever to insult, threaten, and harass. As a result, cyberbullying has become a serious problem for teens everywhere. One in four American teens have been the victim of cyberbullying. Many more have seen it happen to someone they know or have been involved in cyberbullying. If you have been the victim of cyberbullying, you are not alone. There is help available, and there are solutions to the problem.

Opposite: Cyberbullying is a form of repeated harassment that takes place over the internet or via text message.

WHAT IS CYBERBULLYING?

At the most basic level, cyberbullying is using technology, like the internet and cell phones, to bully or harass someone repeatedly. This harassment and bullying can take many different forms. Mean messages, hurtful comments, threats of violence, sharing embarrassing pictures, and pretending to be someone else are some common forms of cyberbullying.

To be classified as cyberbullying, the person responsible must intend to hurt the victim. If the embarrassment or harm is accidental rather than intentional, it is not cyberbullying. For instance, sharing a picture that is embarrassing for one of the people in it without realizing they'll be embarrassed is not cyberbullying. Intentionally sharing the picture to embarrass someone can be cyberbullying.

The definition of traditional, in-person bullying says that harm must occur more than once. The repeated nature of bullying is what makes it different from harassment. Being pushed or insulted once is harassment. When it happens repeatedly, it is bullying. The same is true for cyberbullying. The nature of cyberbullying, however, means that one act can harm someone repeatedly. Publishing a web page that makes fun of someone and leaving it open for comments can cause harm again and again as people look at it. This qualifies it as cyberbullying. Of course, one-time harassment is still a serious matter

Smartphones have connected people more than ever before. Unfortunately, they can also be used to cyberbully.

that can have consequences for both the perpetrator and the victim.

When actions online or on other kinds of technology result in repeated and intentional harm, it is cyberbullying. Most experts agree that it is the intention, repetition, and harm that all add up to cyberbullying. Here are some examples of what this can look like in real life.

Messages and Comments

Sending someone hurtful messages is one of the most frequent ways people are cyberbullied. Often, the messages are mean and tear someone down. They might call the the victim names or belittle them. There are many different platforms where people receive hurtful messages, from social media sites like Facebook and Instagram to text messages and email. Frequently, the bully sends the messages openly, and the victim knows who it is, although occasionally messages are sent anonymously.

Bullying messages may be private or visible to the public. Mean comments on social media are not only hurtful when read by the victim but may also inspire other bullies to post similar abuse. In some cases, these messages may even threaten physical harm. Threats can be traumatizing for the victim and make them fear for their safety at school or even in their home.

Rumors and Gossip

Spreading rumors about someone online or over the phone is another way that cyberbullies can hurt their victims. Rumors and gossip can be spread without the victim's knowledge. Friends and classmates might hear hurtful rumors or insults before a victim is aware that they're being cyberbullied.

Like hurtful messages, rumors can be spread on many different platforms, including group texts and social media. In extreme cases, a cyberbully can even make a website or web page about one or more victims. Rumors, embarrassing photos, and insults might be posted there repeatedly by the cyberbully who made the site—and sometimes by other people as well. According to a 2016 survey by the Cyberbullying Research Center, a shocking 7.4 percent of twelve- to seventeen-year-old students reported that a website created to make fun of them was posted online in the past month.

Photographs and Videos

Cyberbullies sometimes use photographs and videos of a victim to humiliate them. This can be as simple as an unflattering photograph or one where the victim is doing something embarrassing. Posting it online, with or without a hurtful comment, can shame the victim and encourage other people to make fun of them.

A growing problem is the sharing of photos or videos where the victim is partially or fully undressed. These explicit images may have been taken by the victim or with their permission. Either way, when the photos are shared more widely, it is a form of cyberbullying. Spreading explicit images of a person without their consent is a very serious matter and is illegal in many states. It can make the victim feel powerless and betrayed.

Impersonation

Technology affords cyberbullies the opportunity to impersonate, or pretend to be, someone else. Since a cyberbully is hidden behind a screen, it is difficult for the victim—or other people—to tell if someone is being impersonated.

Cyberbullying through impersonation can take many forms. The victim may be impersonated. In this way, the bully can pretend to be the victim and embarrass them or create conflict with people they know. Alternatively, the bully may impersonate someone and then interact with the victim, who thinks they are talking to someone else. The cyberbully might trick the victim into saying something they regret or sending a photograph that is then used to cyberbully them even more.

A CLOSER LOOK AT CYBERBULLYING ON DIGITAL PLATFORMS

Cyberbullying can occur on different digital platforms. Sometimes, it takes place over text message on a phone. More than 95 percent of American teens have a cell phone, which makes them vulnerable to this kind of harassment. According to a 2016 Cyberbullying Research Center poll, 12 percent of teens between the ages of twelve and seventeen reported being threatened with violence via text message in the past month. Cell phone messages can also be used to spread rumors or blackmail a victim.

Any online platform that allows interaction can also be a place where cyberbullying occurs. From chat rooms to online forums, cyberbullying is a threat. The more moderation there is by people trying to prevent abuse, the less the risk to users. Moderation is thorough in some forums or chat rooms and nonexistent in others. Two of the most frequent places cyberbullying occurs are on social media and in video games. Moderation is often lax on these platforms.

Social Media

Social media sites are some of the most common platforms for cyberbullying. Sites like YouTube and

Cyberbullies use social media sites like Instagram to post public messages and send private messages to their victims.

Facebook allow people to form virtual communities and interact with people online, but they also have a dark side. Cyberbullying is widespread on social media, and teens are especially vulnerable to being harassed by friends and strangers alike.

The 2017 Annual Bullying Survey by an anti-bullying organization called Ditch the Label in the United Kingdom asked people between the ages of twelve and twenty-five about their experiences with bullying and cyberbullying. Respondents reported what social media sites they used and if they had ever been cyberbullied or harassed on them. Their answers revealed just how widespread cyberbullying is for people around the world. The following percentages are the number of users who said they had been cyberbullied on a specific social media platform:

- Instagram: 7 percent
- Facebook: 6 percent
- Snapchat: 5 percent
- YouTube: 2 percent

- Twitter: 2 percent

- WhatsApp: 2 percent

- Tumblr: 0 percent

While the degree of the problem depends on the platform, it is clear that cyberbullying is a serious problem on most social media sites. In fact, just 6 percent of people who took the survey answered "yes" to the question, "Are social media sites safe?" The most common response was "it depends," and 14 percent said "no."

Depending on the social media platform, methods of cyberbullying vary. Cyberbullying can be public, such as public comments or tweets, or private, in direct messages. If it is public, it is often meant to shame the victim by having other people see the harassment and perhaps join in. In private, it can be abusive or even criminal. Sometimes, victims are blackmailed. This means they are told that unless they do something, the blackmailer will reveal a photograph or some personal information to everyone. Blackmail is usually done privately since it relies on keeping a secret.

One thirteen-year-old girl from England told her story of being blackmailed to Ditch the Label: "I was on Instagram, and I have a private account. Somebody that I didn't know somehow had a picture of me and said that they would put my face on a nude picture if I didn't answer the call. I didn't answer the call. And to this day I don't know if that person has put it online."

Video Games

Any video game that is multiplayer and allows players to interact has the potential to be used for cyberbullying. In a game setting, cyberbullying may take many different forms. Sometimes, it is done over chat. Players may type offensive and insulting messages aimed at another player. In extreme cases, this can even include death threats. To prevent

Cyberbullying can be vicious in multiplayer video games.

abusive chat messages, some games even disable the option to chat with people who are not friends, but this fails to stop cyberbullying if the victim knows the person responsible.

Depending on the game, other players may be able to harass the victim in different ways. They might kill their in-game character repeatedly or prevent them from enjoying the game in some other way. The hacking of accounts is often a problem for video games. Hacking can even cost the victim money if they have payment options linked to their account.

In 2017, Ditch the Label carried out a survey on gamers between the ages of twelve and twenty-five who used Habbo, a virtual community and game. The survey found that 57 percent of respondents had been cyberbullied while playing a game, 47 percent had been threatened, and 38 percent had been hacked.

Some video games take cyberbullying quite seriously and work to prevent abuse by banning players and limiting player interactions that can be abusive. Other video game makers do very little. If the cyberbully does not know the victim, the victim can usually block them to end the harassment. When the cyberbully knows the victim, however, this can be less effective. The cyberbully can simply turn to social media or some other platform.

COMPARING BULLYING AND CYBERBULLYING

Bullying and cyberbullying are alike in many ways. They are both intentional and repeated acts meant to harm another person. The biggest difference is that bullying takes place in person while cyberbullying takes place through technology. This difference in how they occur leads to some other important differences between bullying and cyberbullying.

No Escape

Bullying usually occurs at school and in other public places. When victims of bullying arrive home, they are usually safe. They can relax with their family and unwind. Even though life may be stressful outside of home, there is somewhere to go to escape.

Victims of cyberbullying are not safe in their own home. No matter where they are, harassment can continue so long as they have their phone with them or they are online. Even if they do not log on, other

Ryan Halligan

Ryan Halligan's father poses with the memorial site he created for his son.

In 2003, cyberbullying was still relatively unknown. The internet had already become a part of daily life for many teens around the world. Instant Messenger, a way to send direct messages to people, and early social media sites were popular, but their risks weren't understood as well as they are today. Ryan Halligan's experience brought media attention to cyberbullying and helped change the way that people think about bullying.

Halligan was attending middle school when a boy started a rumor that he was gay. Then, a girl from school began flirting with Halligan over Instant Messenger and told him that she liked him. It turned out to be a lie. She humiliated Halligan when she told classmates about the prank. Halligan researched suicide methods. He connected with another boy online who was also interested in suicide. When Halligan messaged him to say he was going to kill himself, the boy replied, "The last time i hear u complain? ur finally gonna kill urself?! Its about ... time." Soon after, Halligan took his own life.

After Ryan's death, his father, John Halligan, began working to spread awareness about cyberbullying and suicide to help prevent more deaths. Ryan's story was one of the early, high-profile incidents of cyberbullying. John Halligan worked with lawmakers to get new laws against cyberbullying passed. He also speaks at schools to warn students about the possible consequences of harassing someone online and the devastating effect that suicide has on a family.

people might be making fun of them or spreading rumors online.

This a critical difference between bullying and cyberbullying. Victims of cyberbullying often speak about how they feel constantly harassed and threatened. Even in their own bedroom, they know

Bullying takes place in person, while cyberbullying takes place online.

that another abusive message might be on its way or that people could be spreading more rumors about them.

Online Activity Can Last Forever

Cyberbullying often leaves a trail that is visible for a long time. Abusive comments, web pages made to harass someone, and private pictures posted online can last for years. It can be virtually impossible to erase something from the internet if it spreads far enough in the beginning. This is very different from bullying, which rarely leaves a physical trace that lasts for years.

The permanence of online activity can cause greater distress to victims of cyberbullying. In many cases of cyberbullying, private pictures or videos of the victim are used in the harassment. Often, these pictures are taken by the victim of their own body, but the pictures are meant for one person, not the whole world to see. If these pictures are spread more widely, it can be very difficult to get them off the internet.

This experience does lasting harm to the victim, and many people who experience cyberbullying of this kind talk about the continuing sense of violation because the picture never goes away.

Anonymity

Anonymity allows someone to act without other people being sure who is to blame. The media often claims that only cyberbullies stay anonymous, but this is not the case. Sometimes, in-person bullying is anonymous. Leaving mean messages about someone in their locker or spreading rumors about them in school are examples of in-person bullying done anonymously. The victim may not be sure who is responsible.

Complicating the issue, cyberbullying is often done without anonymity. Many of the most common forms of cyberbullying, like leaving mean comments or making threats, are done openly. Only some forms of cyberbullying are truly anonymous.

Different Audiences

Cyberbullying can happen in front of many more people than traditional bullying does. In a school, bullying usually occurs out of sight since adults would intervene if they saw it. At worst, it might occur in front of a classroom or a hallway full of people. On the other hand, abusive messages and comments online can be viewed by hundreds or even

On many social media sites, users are not required to upload any photos of themselves or enter real information when they sign up. As a result, many cyberbullies stay anonymous.

Myths About Cyberbullying

A common myth about cyberbullying is that it is an epidemic: no one is safe, and most people are cyberbullied. In reality, most people never experience cyberbullying as either the victim or the bully. Cyberbullying is a serious problem that affects many people, but overestimating how often it occurs can lead to a sense of hopelessness. You might think there is nothing to be done about a problem that affects everyone. Nothing could be further from the truth. In reality, there are ways to help put an end to cyberbullying. If you see someone being cyberbullied, you can help. It is not a problem without a solution.

A second related myth is that cyberbullying has become more common than in-person bullying. The opposite is true. Even though schools are trying to combat bullying more than ever before, in-person bullying is still more common than cyberbullying is.

A third myth is that cyberbullies tend to be social outcasts, loners, or kids who are especially mean. This is not the case. According to research and surveys, cyberbullies are often ordinary students. Sometimes, they are quite popular and well-liked in school. Being well-liked and very social doesn't reduce the risk that someone will be a cyberbully. Furthermore, a student with few friends is not more likely to be a cyberbully. The mistaken belief that cyberbullies are exceptional in some way makes it harder to stop cyberbullying. Cyberbullies are kids who have made very hurtful, destructive, and often illegal choices. There is often nothing else to distinguish them from other students.

Similarly, there's no way to easily predict who will be cyberbullied by others. Just because a student is popular does not mean they cannot be bullied by people online.

thousands of people. Sometimes cyberbullying can even go viral and be seen by millions.

Cyberbullying often takes place on platforms without much adult supervision. While schools try to monitor student behavior at all times to prevent bullying, children and teens are often allowed to go online unsupervised at home. Adults typically do not read their private message or texts, and teens may have social media profiles their parents are unaware of. This can make it easier for young people to cyberbully others while hiding it from their parents and the victim's parents.

RAISING AWARENESS

When the internet was still new, there was little public awareness about cyberbullying. Many parents did not know about the risks that the online world posed for their children. High-profile cases of cyberbullying changed this. The deaths of Ryan Halligan and other early victims of cyberbullying were covered by the media. Talk show hosts like Oprah Winfrey and TV news programs examined the issue.

Today, most people know that cyberbullying is a major issue for teens, yet many people do not know details about the risks of cyberbullying and how to put an end to it. The more people know about cyberbullying, the more they can do to stop it. Many schools, students, and adults are working to educate people about cyberbullying. With enough work, cyberbullying may become a problem of the past.

Chapter 2

Real-World Risks

Victims are never to blame for being cyberbullied. The responsibility lies squarely with the cyberbully who harasses, threatens, or blackmails them. Nonetheless, there are some steps that a person can take to minimize their chances of becoming a victim of cyberbullying. Likewise, schools can take measures to protect their students from cyberbullying. Taking these steps to protect teens from cyberbullying is often easier than dealing with cyberbullying once it has begun.

Opposite: Victims of cyberbullies can feel helpless, but there's always someone to turn to.

RISK FACTORS OF VICTIMS

Opportunity is the most important predictor of whether someone will be cyberbullied. Unsupervised time online or on a cell phone gives cyberbullies a chance to take aim. Risk factors like weak adult relationships and sharing passwords put students with unsupervised time online at an even greater risk for victimization. Still, it is important to remember that whether a person is subject to some or all these risk factors does not mean they are responsible for being cyberbullied. The blame for cyberbullying rests on the cyberbullies alone—not their victim.

Time Online

How time spent online relates to cyberbullying is a controversial subject. Researchers have tried to answer this question for years with somewhat contradictory results. In 2012, a study by University of Washington Seattle researchers Katie Davis and Lucas Koepke found no relationship between a person's time spent online and their risk of being cyberbullied. However, they did find that adolescents who spent more time on their cell phones were at greater risk of receiving threatening and harassing text messages.

A different 2012 study published in *Children and Youth Services Review* looked at 2,186 surveys completed by high-school and middle-school students. It found that students who reported being the victim of cyberbullying were also likely to spend more time online than their peers. This contradicted the findings of Davis and Koepke. In 2018, a further scientific study was published by *BMC Public Health*. In this study, researchers found that spending more than two hours a day on social media increased the chance that teens in Europe would become victims of cyberbullying.

Weak Adult Relationships

Students who do not have a strong relationship with any adults are at greater risk of being cyberbullied. They do not have anyone to turn to if they run into problems online. This is also a major risk factor for in-person bullying.

On the other hand, students who do have a good relationship with their parents or another adult figure, like a coach or teacher, are less likely to be cyberbullied. If they do become the victim of cyberbullying, they are much better at dealing with it constructively. They have someone to turn to for advice and help putting an end to the cyberbullying. They are also much less likely to experience severe negative effects of cyberbullying like fear, depression, and self-harm.

Sharing Passwords

Cyberbullies and their victims are more likely to share online passwords than other students, according to surveys. This is one issue that students have a great deal of control over. It is never a good idea to share your passwords with someone other than a parent or guardian or when it is required by a school. Your online accounts should have different passwords too.

Never share your passwords with friends. Doing so puts you at risk.

That way, if someone learns your password to one account, they cannot access your other accounts.

Sharing passwords allows other people to impersonate you. Even if you trust a person, your relationship with them may one day change. They could also give your password to someone else on purpose or by accident. Impersonation is a very serious issue when it comes to cyberbullying. When someone can send messages that appear to come from you, they can destroy your relationships with other people and spread rumors easily.

RISK FACTORS OF CYBERBULLIES

In the effort to end cyberbullying, some research has been done on what characteristics cyberbullies tend to share. Thus far, researchers have found relatively few risk factors that put a teen at risk of becoming a cyberbully. It is important to remember that people who have one—or all—of these risk factors aren't guaranteed to become a cyberbully. Likewise, many cyberbullies do not have any of these identified risk factors.

Low Parental Supervision

The main risk factor for both cyberbullies and bullies is a low level of parental supervision. The parents of bullies tend not to monitor what they do. This is not surprising. Most parents would try to stop their child from being a bully or cyberbully if they were aware of the problem. When parents do not supervise their child, they are often left in the dark about the bullying the child engages in.

A lack of parental supervision can also be a symptom of a larger problem in the family. Students who face problems at home like conflict and drug use are more likely to bully or cyberbully others. Nonetheless, many cyberbullies live in families that are not dysfunctional in any way.

Family Violence

According to a study by Sabina Low and Dorothy L. Espelage, higher levels of family violence increase

Many experts think that a major risk factor for becoming a cyberbully or being cyberbullied is how much unsupervised time you spend online.

Adults and Cyberbullying

Elementary-, middle-, and high-school students are usually the focus when it comes to cyberbullying. Efforts to tackle the issue focus on schools, students, and parents. Victims of cyberbullying who receive widespread media attention are almost always in this age group. Nonetheless, cyberbullying affects adults as well.

Megan Meier took her own life after being cyberbullied by a classmate's mother.

There are a few studies on how widespread cyberbullying is once a person graduates from high school. These studies show that cyberbullying after high school is surprisingly common. Students in colleges, and even adults in workplaces, can endure cyberbullying from people in their life. Any adult online can also be the target of cyberbullies they do not know in real life. Many of the tips and strategies in this book apply to adults as much as to teens.

In some cases, adults can even cyberbully teens. Thirteen-year-old Megan Meier was targeted by the mother of one of her classmates. Lori Drew impersonated a sixteen-year-old boy on the social media website MySpace. After befriending Meier with the false profile, she began harassing Meier and writing abusive posts that other people could see. Upset and distraught by the cyberbullying, Meier killed herself.

Drew escaped responsibility for her actions because cyberbullying laws did not exist at the time in Missouri. Meier's mother started an organization in Megan's honor to combat bullying, cyberbullying, and suicide.

the risk someone will cyberbully others. Their study looked at 1,023 adolescents in the fifth, sixth, and seventh grades to come to this conclusion. Family violence refers not only to acts like shoving and hitting, but also to shouting and yelling. Students who lived in households where this sort of behavior is common are more likely to engage in nonphysical bullying, like cyberbullying.

As research continues into risk factors for cyberbullying, it may become a useful tool in the struggle to end it. A better understanding of what makes someone cyberbully others may make it easier to reach potential bullies and put a stop to their negative actions. As of now, this research is still in its early stages.

EXPLICIT PHOTOGRAPHS

Cyberbullying is often entangled with another activity that some teens engage in: sending nude or explicit photographs of themselves. This is extremely risky behavior and can have wide-ranging consequences for everyone involved. According to research published in *JAMA Pediatrics* in 2018, sending explicit photographs is a big problem in schools. Data from 110,380 children between the ages of twelve and eighteen showed that nearly 15 percent had sent nude photographs of themselves to someone else, and 27 percent had received such an image. Additionally, 12 percent of teens had forwarded an explicit image of someone they knew without that person's consent.

There are many issues that surround this high-risk behavior. Judges and courts in the United States have sometimes ruled that when someone under the age of eighteen takes nude images of themselves, those images count as child pornography. Therefore, if someone under the age of eighteen takes a picture of themselves and sends it to someone else, both people are in possession of child pornography. Possession of child pornography is a serious crime that can result in fines, jail time, and being added to the official registry of sex offenders. If you are convicted of possessing child pornography, it can affect the rest of your life. For this reason, it is a terrible idea to take explicit photographs of yourself—or ask for, or view, such photographs of others.

Beyond legal consequences, explicit photographs are often used in cases of cyberbullying. Frequently, an image is taken in the context of a romantic relationship between two teens, and it is not meant to be seen by anyone else. Nonetheless, the image may be shared beyond its intended recipient. This may happen intentionally after a breakup, accidentally, or when someone else accesses a phone or device that has the image on it.

Once an image is out in the world, it can be impossible to ever really erase it from the internet. Many times, the image is then used to cyberbully the person who took it. This is what happened to Amanda Todd, a girl from Canada. When she was just twelve years old, an older man convinced her to briefly lift her shirt up as they video chatted. Without her knowledge, he took a screenshot.

The screenshot haunted the rest of her life. The man, Aydin Coban, used the image to blackmail and harass her before spreading it to her classmates over Facebook. People she knew in real life joined in the abuse and harassed her as well, even assaulting her at school. After enduring years of cyberbullying, Amanda Todd died by suicide in 2012 at the age of fifteen. She left behind a moving YouTube video of how the harassment made her feel. Viewed more than seventeen million times, her courageous video has helped spread awareness of the harm of cyberbullying.

The tragic case of Amanda Todd highlights how women and girls are often targets of cyberbullying. Cyberbullies shame or harass women based on assumptions about their sexuality. Harassing comments may include calling someone's clothing too revealing or guessing about the number of relationships someone has had in the past.

The clothing, appearance, and actions of girls and women is often criticized and analyzed by people who

Mourners gather at a memorial for Amanda Todd, who died by suicide in 2012 after being cyberbullied.

have no right to do so. This can rise to the level of harassment and cyberbullying in many cases. Nude photographs of a person can add fuel to the fire.

Taking nude photographs of yourself makes you vulnerable to cyberbullying. It is never a good idea to take such photographs for this reason—as well as the fact that it is illegal in many states if you are under the age of eighteen.

HIGH-RISK GROUPS

Researchers are still trying to understand the complex relationship between certain groups and their likelihood of being cyberbullied. Awareness that certain groups are more likely to be cyberbullied can encourage friends, school staff, and parents to keep an eye out for signs of cyberbullying.

Students with disabilities, including physical or intellectual disabilities as well as conditions like autism spectrum disorder, are at a much greater risk for bullying. Students with disabilities or special needs make up roughly 15 percent of the school-age population. The exact percentage varies by country. Despite how common disabilities and special needs are, students with disabilities are often singled out for bullying and cyberbullying.

LGBTQ (lesbian, gay, bisexual, transgender, queer) students are much more likely to be bullied or cyberbullied as well. Even students who are perceived to be part of the LGBTQ community are at increased risk, regardless of their actual sexual orientation and gender identity. Like students with disabilities, LGBTQ students are at higher risk of bullying due to the perception that they are "different" from other students.

When this perception exists and leads to bullying or cyberbullying, it is a major failing in the school system. Schools need to ensure that they create a safe environment for all students, including students with disabilities and LGBTQ students. To do so, it is essential to challenge bigotry and stereotypes.

SCHOOLS AND CYBERBULLYING

While students themselves can take steps to protect themselves from cyberbullying, schools are at the forefront of anti-cyberbullying efforts. It is up to schools to create a safe climate where bullying and cyberbullying are not tolerated. There are many different ways school systems can do this, and the stakes are high. When schools fail, cyberbullying can spread unchecked.

Analysis by the Cyberbullying Research Center found that school climate affected cyberbullying— even cyberbullying that took place off school property.

A school in Yuma, Arizona, holds an anti-bullying assembly.

In schools where students felt safe and respected, children and teens were much less likely to cyberbully others, be victims of cyberbullying, or send or receive explicit photos. The benefits of having a safe school environment lasted all day for students.

Schools can also take steps to educate students and staff about cyberbullying: what it is and how to

ReThink

Trisha Prabhu is one teen who decided to make a difference. When she was just thirteen years old, she heard about other kids who had died by suicide after being cyberbullied. Inspired to try to help, she developed ReThink. ReThink is freely available software that helps people choose not to post offensive messages.

ReThink detects when someone has typed out a hurtful message. Before the message goes through, ReThink asks them if they really want to say what they typed. Amazingly, 93 percent of the time, the author of the offensive message decides not to post it. ReThink does not censor students, forbidding them from writing something. Instead, it gives them a chance to rethink their actions, and usually people make the right choice when they are given this opportunity.

ReThink also works with schools to help end cyberbullying. Trisha Prabhu speaks at events about the terrible effects of online abuse and harassment. Rather than watch in silence as people were cyberbullied, she chose to act. Her work is a reminder that each one of us can make a difference if we decide to.

Trisha Prabhu received a WebMD Health Hero award in 2016 for her anti-cyberbullying software, ReThink.

stop it. Awareness campaigns have been known to effectively combat cyberbullying and decrease how often it occurs. When cyberbullies are educated about the enormous harm that cyberbullying can do, they will sometimes stop cyberbullying.

Yet when cyberbullying between students does not stop after school-wide programs, it is the responsibility of school administrators to stop it. Many schools have anonymous ways to report cyberbullying. A victim or a bystander can report harassment or cyberbullying so that the school can step in.

WHAT YOU CAN DO

The risks for cyberbullying reveal some actions that students can take to protect themselves. First, it is never a good idea to take or share explicit photographs of yourself or other students. Explicit images are often used to blackmail or cyberbully someone if the images are later forwarded to people who were not meant to see them. Also, if the person in the image is under the age of eighteen, possessing or sharing that photo is illegal. Second, you should never share passwords with someone other than a parent or in situations where it is required by your school's policy. Third, you should try to find an adult at school you can trust and talk to if you can't talk openly with your parent or guardian. If you ever need to report cyberbullying or discuss problems you are having, this will give you someone to turn to.

Victims of cyberbullying are not to blame if they made the mistake of taking photos of themselves or sharing passwords, and some people are cyberbullied despite being very careful online. Parents, the school community, or law enforcement can help victims, depending on the specific case.

Chapter 3

Experiencing Cyberbullying

many people are affected by cyberbullying. In any instance of cyberbullying, there is always a victim and one or more cyberbullies. Additionally, there may be bystanders who either decide to join in the harassment, do nothing, or defend the victim. The experiences of these different groups are often quite different, and they're important to understand.

Opposite: No one should have to endure threatening or harassing messages. Make sure to tell an adult you trust if it happens to you.

VICTIMS OF CYBERBULLYING

When someone is cyberbullied, they may experience all sorts of negative feelings and consequences. The longer the cyberbullying lasts and the more intense it is, the greater these effects. This is why it is important to try to stop the cyberbullying as soon as possible. It's critical to tell an adult immediately, whether you are a target or someone you know is being cyberbullied.

The following issues are some of the most common effects that victims of cyberbullying must deal with. Keep in mind that people respond to stressful situations in different ways, and many victims will experience just some of these effects.

Social Isolation

Teens who are cyberbullied report feelings of isolation from people around them. It is unsurprising that teens feel disconnected from classmates who are involved in the cyberbullying and those who stand by without

Social isolation is just one negative effect of cyberbullying.

doing anything. However, victims of cyberbullying also report that they feel isolated from their parents, families, and friends who are not involved in their harassment at all.

Social isolation relates to other issues that victims of cyberbullying often deal with: low self-esteem, a loss of trust in other people, and greater social anxiety. Low self-esteem means that a person feels incompetent, awkward, or not worthy of love. Social anxiety is a feeling of unease or stress in social situations with other people. The experience of being harassed repeatedly, often in front of people who do nothing to help or step in, makes the victim lose faith in themselves and others. That's why cyberbullying leads to low self-esteem, less trust, and social anxiety.

Depression and Suicidal Thoughts

Victims of cyberbullying often experience many negative psychological effects. Depression—a medical illness marked by sadness and a loss of interest in activities that once seemed fun—is common in victims. Studies have found that the more intensely someone is cyberbullied, the greater their symptoms of depression tend to be. Depression can involve feelings of hopelessness and powerlessness as well as simple sadness and disinterest.

Depression is a risk factor for suicide. Being cyberbullied is an additional risk factor for suicide, above and beyond any depression it may cause. In fact, cyberbullying puts someone at greater risk for suicide than in-person bullying does. Victims of cyberbullying attempt suicide nearly twice as frequently as their peers.

Lower Grades

According to studies and surveys, victims of cyberbullying sometimes see their academic performance suffer. In fact, some studies have found that victims of cyberbullying receive lower grades than victims of other kinds of bullying.

Poor academic performance may be due to a number of causes. The stress, depression, and social isolation of being a victim may make it difficult to focus on or complete schoolwork. Experiencing such a traumatic event may shift a student's priorities away from learning. Additionally, many victims of cyberbullying miss school more frequently than their peers. Fears of being harassed in class or having to see people who cyberbully them may lead them to skip classes or find ways to avoid going to school.

Natalie's Story

One victim of cyberbullying who went on the record about her experience is Natalie Farzanek. She spoke to Patrick Sawyer, a reporter at the *Guardian*, about the effects that cyberbullying had on her. Farzanek's story began when she signed up with Facebook and other social media sites. She had been bullied in person at school, but she always felt safe at home. That changed when she began using social media. Her tormenters from school started targeting her online as well. Farzanek described how the harassment started and how it made her feel:

I got messages from people telling me to kill myself and saying that the world would be better off without me and that everybody hated me. Soon I was diagnosed with depression and anxiety. I lost all self-esteem and became paranoid about people. I couldn't trust anyone because I found out that even some of the people who had been nice to me at school had begun to send me abusive messages anonymously online. At one stage, I even began to feel suicidal, and I started to self-harm. The problem with cyberbullying is that it's done in the comfort of your own home, and there's nowhere to escape to.

Natalie reported the problem to the social media sites, but they never responded. Eventually, she became active in helping other victims of cyberbullying through charities and local groups. She credits this activism with boosting her self-esteem, and the cyberbullying eventually stopped. Natalie is now a motivational speaker and tries to help others dealing with cyberbullying and the many negative effects it can have on victims.

THE EXPERIENCE OF CYBERBULLIES

Like their victims, cyberbullies tend to have more problems in their lives than other students. They are more likely to experience a number of behavioral and emotional issues than the average student. Research into the experience of cyberbullies, however, is still in its early days. Often, surveys and data do not measure if the issues that cyberbullies face *result* from their online behavior or *cause* their online behavior. This issue is a major problem with interpreting data that is often called "correlation versus causation."

Correlation means that when one situation happens it often takes place at the same time as a second situation, but one of the situations does not cause the other one. Causation means that one thing causes another to happen. For instance, data suggests that being cyberbullied causes some people to become depressed.

One famous example of correlation is several studies that linked murder rates to ice cream sales: the more ice cream that was sold in a time period, the more people were murdered. Of course, researchers never thought that buying ice cream turned someone into a murderer. It was an example of correlation, not causation. After more research, experts suspect the real link is that hot weather drives both ice cream sales and increased crime.

The relationship between cyberbullying and issues like alcohol use is still being studied. It is possible that drinking alcohol makes a person slightly more likely to cyberbully through lowering their self-control. It is also possible cyberbullies tend to drink more out of remorse. These would be causal relationships. Nonetheless, it is also possible that drinking alcohol and cyberbullying are just correlated. There may not be a causal relationship at all. Teens struggling with other issues may just be at risk for both cyberbullying and using alcohol.

Alcohol and Drug Use

The strength of the link between cyberbullying and alcohol and drug use is still being investigated. Studies have been conducted in different countries

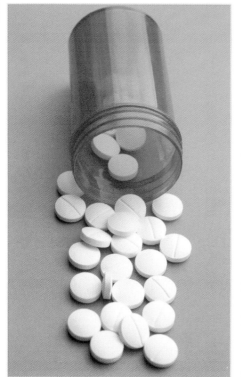

Researchers are studying the link between drug use and bullying.

and across different age ranges with mixed results. Some small studies showed that students who drink alcohol and use drugs are more likely to be cyberbullies, while others did not show this relationship. It is also not clear if alcohol and drug use usually occurs before someone begins cyberbullying or as a result of a person cyberbullying.

Larger studies have been done on traditional bullying. One example from Chile gathered data from 36,687 students across 756 schools in the Latin American country. It found that both bullies and victims of bullying were more likely to smoke cigarettes, drink alcohol, and do drugs than other students.

Studies investigating whether this is also the case in cyberbullying have been smaller and not as conclusive. Researchers think there is likely some relationship between alcohol and drug use and cyberbullying, but there need to be more studies to be sure. Regardless of whether causation or correlation is at play, experts know that tackling issues like alcohol use leads to happier and healthier teens.

Behavioral and Emotional Problems

Cyberbullies are more likely than their peers to experience several emotional and behavioral issues. Like their victims, they are prone to low self-esteem and depression. This can negatively affect their mood and their quality of life. Delinquency is also a concern for cyberbullies as well as their victims.

Unlike their victims, cyberbullies are also prone to more serious behavioral problems. They are more likely to destroy other people's property and commit crimes than other adolescents. This increased risk of criminal behavior is in addition

Canadian Cyberbullying Laws

Some countries around the world have much stricter laws about cyberbullying than the United States does. In Canada, schools and the police are given a great deal of leeway in how they handle the problem. This gives them the ability to help victims of cyberbullying— and punish cyberbullies— to a greater degree than their American counterparts.

As in the United States, laws in Canada vary by province. (Canada is divided into provinces in the same way the United States is divided into states.) The province

This map shows Canadian provinces. Each Canadian province has different laws surrounding cyberbullying.

of Alberta, home to the city of Calgary, has some of the strictest cyberbullying laws. Students who witness cyberbullying but fail to report it can face suspension or expulsion from school.

Many provinces in Canada allow the school to get involved in cases of cyberbullying, even if it is not done on school grounds. If a student goes home and harasses another student online, their school can still hold them responsible for their actions. This avoids a major issue in the United States: when harassment occurs outside of school, the school is legally unable to interfere.

In Canada, there is also a nationwide law that tackles the issue of sharing explicit photographs of another person— an issue that often appears in cyberbullying cases. If someone shares an explicit photograph without the consent of the person pictured, they can face serious consequences, including up to five years in prison. While some American states have similar laws, others do not. Strict laws like those in Canada make it easier to put a stop to cyberbullying.

to cyberbullying, which is a crime in most areas. High levels of aggression, like picking fights, are also found in cyberbullies more frequently than in the general population.

One study published in the *Journal of Youth and Adolescence* found that these behavioral and emotional problems often occurred before cyberbullying. The study found that ninth and tenth graders who had low self-esteem, symptoms of depression, and aggression were more likely to be cyberbullies in the eleventh grade.

Stories of Cyberbullies

There are many reasons why people choose to cyberbully someone else. These reasons have little to do with the victim of the cyberbullying, and much more to do with the cyberbully. Answering the question of what motivates cyberbullies is quite difficult. The cyberbully may not fully understand their own motivations. Nonetheless, researchers have tried to answer the question.

Professor Kris Varjas and her colleagues interviewed twenty high school students and asked them questions about why they thought students cyberbullied and harassed each other online. The students identified many different motivations, including boredom, attempts to protect themselves from being the subject of similar harassment, and a desire for attention or approval from their peers.

Occasionally, revenge or jealousy also motivates cyberbullies. According to Tyler Gregory, who spoke

Cyberbullies are more likely to destroy others' property than their peers.

to radio station WBUR about cyberbullying, this is what motivated him and his friends to target a girl they did not even know. He was part of a group of five boys who always hung out together in junior high school, when one boy began spending more and more time with a girl. This made the four friends jealous, and they decided to get revenge online:

And so, you know, the four of us, we kind of went on social media and took out our frustration toward this girl whom we had never met. And, looking back, I'm like, "How in the world would I have been able to have said some of those things?" You know, we talked about her weight. We talked about her appearance, and really just to make her feel bad. I think it really stems from, you know, cyberbullying ... you're not face-to-face with the person you're bullying. It makes it a lot easier. You're not seeing the reaction, if there is a reaction. You're not, you know, giving them an opportunity to necessarily retaliate unless they message you back or comment on something like that.

The harassment stopped only when one of the boys told the girl to kill herself. They realized that her harming herself was a possibility and decided to stop. Their former friend had also gotten involved in telling them to stop the harassment when he found out about it.

Sometimes, the cyberbully is trying to make themselves feel better and redirect their own negative feelings and emotions toward someone else. This is why Landon Eason used to go into internet chat rooms and harass other users. She told her story to a local Saint Louis television station, 5 On Your Side:

If I found somebody that I thought would retaliate or respond, and if I had an opportunity, I would just pounce. I was hoping it would make me feel like I was superior to them. That was the thing. That was the thing. Because I was made to feel worthless my entire life. What I was doing was I was telling them what I wish I could say to the people who bullied me.

Eventually, Eason realized that cyberbullying others did not make her feel better about herself. She sought help from a therapist and worked through her problems without trying to victimize others. In the end, she stopped cyberbullying other people online.

BULLY-VICTIMS

So far, we have looked at cyberbullies and their victims as two different groups. This is how it works for most adolescents involved with cyberbullying: they are either the victim or the cyberbully. However, a third group, bully-victims, still make up a significant number of teens involved in cyberbullying. Bully-victims cyberbully other adolescents while also being the victims of cyberbullying themselves. According to studies, about 20 percent of adolescents involved in cyberbullying are bully-victims.

Bully-victims are more negatively affected by cyberbullying than those who are either victims or bullies alone. Bully-victims experience the downsides of both groups, from depression and social isolation to substance use. They are also more likely to attempt suicide than victims or cyberbullies are.

If you or someone you know is a bully-victim, there is help available. Even though you have cyberbullied other people, you still deserve help. Talking to a trusted adult about the problem is the first step; this could include a parent, trusted teacher, or school counselor. Breaking the cycle of being a bully-victim

To start healing from the effects of cyberbullying, reach out to a teacher, parent, or school guidance counselor.

One Teen's Fight Against Cyberbullying

Jessica Logan's mother speaks to Ohio lawmakers about the Jessica Logan Act.

Jessica Logan's experience of cyberbullying began when she broke up with her boyfriend. Like nearly half of American teens, she had sent explicit photographs of herself to him while they were dating. Angry after their breakup, he spread those pictures around their high school. Logan was devastated. Some of her classmates began harassing her and calling her names. She started skipping school due to the endless abuse.

The cyberbullying lasted for months. Logan and her parents went to her school's administration, but the school offered little help. Finally, Logan went to the local media with her story. She detailed her experience and the harassment she suffered, saying, "I just want to make sure no one else will have to go through this again." Afterward, Logan's parents thought the worst was over. She seemed to be her old self again. Just two months after the interview, one of Logan's friends died by suicide. After the funeral, Logan took her own life. She was just eighteen years old.

Logan's parents continued her legacy of fighting against cyberbullying. They worked tirelessly to spread awareness about the dangers of cyberbullying. In 2012, their efforts paid off with the passage of the Jessica Logan Act in her home state of Ohio. The new law requires schools to ban cyberbullying and have policies in place to combat cyberbullying.

can greatly help how you feel and reduce depression, isolation, and stress.

STOPPING THE CYCLE

Cyberbullies, their victims, and bully-victims all experience many negative effects in their lives.

Though victims of cyberbullying are not responsible for these negative effects, the same cannot be said for cyberbullies. There is no doubt

Everyone deserves to feel safe online.

that being a cyberbully is wrong. Schools and law enforcement need to strictly enforce efforts to stop cyberbullying and make cyberbullies take responsibility for their actions when they are caught.

Nonetheless, cyberbullies also need help to stop their destructive behavior. Helping cyberbullies and bully-victims means fewer people will be cyberbullied in the future. Their own lives will also improve as the negative effects associated with being a cyberbully fade. Cyberbullies like Tyler Gregory and Landon Eason report being happier after they stopped cyberbullying.

Chapter 4

Hope and Recovery

Being the victim of cyberbullying can make you feel hopeless and alone. It may feel like the harassment and bullying will never end. This is a normal feeling, but it is far from the truth. There are many people who can help you, and the cyberbullying will end one day. Don't give up; there is always hope.

SIGNS OF CYBERBULLYING

If you are being cyberbullied, it is usually easy to tell. Threatening texts, harassment on social media, and

Opposite: Recovering from the effects of cyberbullying can be hard work, but you can and will recover.

threats to expose embarrassing pictures or videos are all straightforward cases of cyberbullying. Whether you know the cyberbully or they remain anonymous, all these acts are clear-cut examples of cyberbullying.

In some cases, the line between cyberbullying and teasing may be blurrier. Sometimes, friends may post comments that are not meant to be upsetting or pictures that they did not notice were embarrassing. If it is the first time a friend has done this, you may want to talk to them privately before assuming they are being a cyberbully. These situations are usually easy to resolve since no harm was intended. When harm is intended, rude comments and teasing rise to the level of cyberbullying.

While it is usually clear if you are being cyberbullied, it can be much harder to tell if a friend is being cyberbullied. They may be embarrassed by the situation and try to hide it from others. Unless the cyberbullying is done publicly, for example on social media, you may never know what they are going through.

There are warning signs that someone may be being cyberbullied. Their behavior may change. If a friend starts to refuse to leave their house or go out in public, it may be a sign. They may also stop sleeping or eating as much, and their grades may fall. They might seem less interested in school and activities that they used to enjoy.

Many of these symptoms are similar to the symptoms of other common problems among adolescents, like depression and drug use, so these signs alone are not enough to suspect cyberbullying. Cyberbullying, however, has additional signs that revolve around technology. If your friend seems anxious, agitated, or sad after looking at their phone or computer, it could be a sign of cyberbullying. Suddenly deleting social media accounts or not using technology as much—or far more than usual—is another sign. If you suspect your friend is being cyberbullied, try to be supportive. You can ask them if anything is wrong or if they want to talk about anything.

HELPING A FRIEND

If your friend is being cyberbullied, one of the most important things you can do is just support them and be there for them. Remind them that it is not their fault they are being cyberbullied, no matter what they have done, and let them know they can tell you how they feel. You may also give them advice about what to do if they are open to it.

Your friends may even ask you to help them speak to an adult or report the problem. If this happens, you can be a great help to them. However, do not try to speak for them, and unless you think they are in serious trouble, you should ask them for permission before reporting the harassment to the school or police. If you think they are in danger of harming themselves, you should tell an adult immediately.

If you know the cyberbullies, you can ask them to stop cyberbullying your friend if you can do so safely. Likewise, you can stand up for your friends on social media if the harassment is occurring there.

Your actions may cause other people to stand up for your friend too. If you do not think you can stand up to cyberbullies safely, you can privately message your friend that you do not agree with the cyberbullies. This will keep them from feeling alone or like everyone is watching and no one supports them.

HELPING YOURSELF

Responding correctly to cyberbullying can be tricky. Depending on the situation, it may be best to select one of many different options. We will look at some of the most common responses that people take to put an end to cyberbullying. Some of these responses help in some situations and not in others. It is always a good idea to talk to a trusted adult about being the victim of cyberbullying. They can help you decide what to do next and remind you that you are not to blame.

When responding to cyberbullying, it is important to remember not to escalate the situation by responding aggressively. It may be tempting to respond with mean comments of your own if someone starts cyberbullying you. However, this will just complicate the situation. Often, cyberbullies are looking for a response. The angrier you get, the more they will attack you. Additionally, if you need to go your school administration or the police later, your own actions may come back to haunt you. Regardless of who started it, the school may look at your response as cyberbullying or harassment if it is aggressive.

It is also important to save a record of the cyberbullying if you are a victim. Do not immediately delete messages or texts. If you ever need to talk to your school or the police about the cyberbullying, this record will help a great deal.

Blocking and Ignoring the Cyberbullies

The first step to stopping cyberbullying is usually blocking the cyberbullies. If they are texting or calling, you can block their number on your cell phone. If the

Nearly every digital platform lets you block other users.

cyberbullying is on social media or in a game, most platforms have the option to block the cyberbully's messages from showing up. At the same time, it is usually best to ignore any messages that might have gotten through before they were blocked. Responses are likely to encourage further harassment.

The Cyberbullying Research Center conducted a survey of teens and asked them what steps they took that successfully stopped them from being cyberbullied more. Nearly a third said that they blocked the cyberbullies, and that was a successful solution. A seventeen-year-old girl from New Jersey responded to the survey with her experience blocking cyberbullies:

Based on my experience, the best action was to simply block that person ... Followed by a nice chat with a good friend, to talk out how it affected me and why, then put it behind me.

About 19 percent said that ignoring the cyberbullies stopped the harassment. While this is a good strategy, it should usually be paired with a more proactive approach as well, such as talking to a trusted adult and blocking the accounts or phone numbers of the cyberbullies.

Telling a Parent

Many teens also reported that telling their parents about the cyberbullying put an end to it. It is always a good idea to talk to a parent or trusted adult about cyberbullying. Even if you do not want them to intervene, they can support you and offer advice. If a parent does intervene, they can talk to the school

Talk to your parents if you are being cyberbullied. There are actions they can take to help you.

administration, the parents of the cyberbullies, or the police.

Talking to the school is usually the first step for a parent to take. Schools are often required to have cyberbullying policies and plans in place for how to deal with the situation. While some schools may not be helpful in cyberbullying situations, more and more schools are taking responsibility for protecting their students from cyberbullying.

The wisdom of talking to a cyberbully's parents is debated by experts. Sometimes, the parents may help put an end to the harassment, but on occasion, they are unhelpful. They may even become combative or angry, so talking to parents you do not know can be risky. However, if your parents have a relationship with the parents of the cyberbully and think they would listen, talking to them can put an end to the cyberbullying. This was the experience of one sixteen-year-old girl who responded to the Cyberbullying Research Center survey:

My parents talked with the parents of the other student. My parents encouraged me to block the student and to change my screen name and passwords. I think the fact that my parents called the other student's parents and went right to the source helped.

Whether to talk to the parents of the cyberbully is a personal decision for you and your parents to make.

Reporting the Cyberbully

If the cyberbullying is occurring on social media or in a game, you can report the cyberbullies. The digital platform will usually ban cyberbullies if there is evidence of abusive chat messages or abusive behavior. Occasionally, websites do not take complaints seriously, but this is becoming less and less common as people hold social media sites responsible for what occurs on their platforms.

If nothing else works, you may need to report the cyberbullying to the police. A trusted adult should be able to help you do this. Make sure you bring a record of the cyberbullying, such as old messages.

While knowledge about cyberbullying is growing, some police departments will do more than others. The response of the police depends a great deal on the individual officers or department. There have been cases where police proved unhelpful, but often

It's always a good idea to set your social media and gaming accounts to "private."

they can intervene and stop the cyberbullying if they know who is to blame.

Privacy Settings and Online Safety

Whether you are the victim of cyberbullying or not, you should change your online privacy settings to protect yourself. Make sure that strangers cannot view or post to your social media or gaming accounts. Additionally, do not accept friend requests from people you do not know. These measures prevent both strangers and classmates from using throwaway accounts to harass you.

It is also important that you never give out personal information on the internet, even to people who you think are your friends. Your relationship with them could sour at some point in the future. It is best if people you meet online do not know your real name, phone number, personal address, city of residence, or school you attend. Nor should they have access to your social media accounts that have this information. It is often very easy to use

The National Suicide Prevention Hotline

If you or someone you know is thinking about hurting themselves, there is always help available. In the United States, you can call the National Suicide Prevention hotline twenty-four hours a day at 1-800-273-8255. A counselor is waiting to take your call and help you through whatever you are facing. Even if you are emotionally distressed and not necessarily suicidal, you can get help by calling.

Calling the hotline is free and confidential, so there is no need to worry about the cost or that your privacy will be violated. A counselor can talk about your problems and how you are having trouble coping. They can also recommend nearby services, so you can get help close to where you live. If you are in serious emotional distress or thinking of harming yourself, don't hesitate to call.

If you live in Canada, Canada Suicide Prevention Services offers a similar hotline that is free and confidential. Their number is 1-833-456-4566. Calling can be the first step to feeling better and learning about other ways to find support.

one piece of information to learn everything about someone. Once someone knows your full identity, cyberbullying and harassment are nearly impossible to stop. It can start happening across all your online accounts and via text messages.

Treatment for Victims

If you or someone you know has been the target of cyberbullying, reach out to professionals who can help you. It is normal to feel anxious and depressed after such a traumatizing experience. Talking to someone about your feelings can help you overcome the negative effects of being cyberbullied.

A school counselor may be able to help you, depending on the circumstances. Otherwise, a therapist or counselor outside of school can work with you. You will need the help of a trusted adult to get an appointment. In most cities, there are counselors or therapists who will help you even if you do not have health insurance or the money to pay them.

A therapist can help you move forward from the cyberbullying you've experienced.

Seeing a mental health professional is not a sign of weakness. It is the first step to feeling better. If you suffer from depression, anxiety, or low self-esteem after being cyberbullied, they will be able to help you.

HELPING A CYBERBULLY

If your friend is a cyberbully, you may be able to get them to stop. If you can do so safely without them lashing out at you, talk to your friend about cyberbullying and how serious it is. A cyberbully may listen to a close friend who explains the harm their actions can cause. If you are very close to a cyberbully, you may even want to advise them to talk to an adult about their actions. School counselors may be able to help them stop their behavior if they find it difficult to do so.

Cyberbullies, like their victims, think that their actions are approved of by their peers when nobody stands up to them and tells them to stop. By talking to a friend who is a cyberbully, you can show them that people disapprove. They will be less likely to cyberbully in the future. This is one reason it so important not to be a silent bystander to cyberbullying.

BEING AN UPSTANDER, NOT A BYSTANDER

In most cases of cyberbullying, there are bystanders who witness the cyberbullying as it occurs. On social media, these are people who view the cyberbully's

Justice for Victims of Cyberbullying

Cyberbullies who are not helped when they are young can go on to cyberbully dozens of victims over the course of their lives. This does great harm to their victims and makes the world a worse place. When a cyberbully is caught, they must face the consequences of their actions.

In a great victory for justice, the predator who first targeted Amanda Todd was caught in the Netherlands. He was the person who took explicit pictures of Amanda Todd and used them to blackmail her before distributing them online, actions that eventually led to her suicide. Aydin Coban went on trial for his actions against not just Amanda Todd, but also many more victims. In 2017, he was sentenced to ten years in prison for his crimes, including blackmail and fraud. He faces more charges in both Canada and the Netherlands.

While Coban was responsible for one of the worst cyberbullying cases in recent years, his harsh sentence is an example of how cyberbullies can be held accountable.

Aydin Coban, the cyberbully who preyed on Amanda Todd and many other girls, was tried in this Amsterdam courthouse in 2017.

Just because someone posts something anonymously online does not mean they will not have to confront their actions one day in court.

If you are able to, you should say something to a friend who is cyberbullying others.

posts. Bystanders are one of the reasons that targets of cyberbullying feel so bad about the harassment. They know that many of their friends and classmates see their situation, yet most do not do anything to stop it.

One tenth grader named Lucia shared her story of being cyberbullied with the Cybersmile Foundation. She recalled how it made her feel when bystanders did not stand up for her:

> I was scared and devastated when students from my grade who I thought were my friends commented about how funny [the cyberbully] was and how annoying I was. People from other schools that I didn't know even chimed in! I felt attacked and all alone. My close friends tried to comfort me privately, but no one had the courage to actually defend me on social media. I had this horrible sinking feeling of everyone hating me and talking about me behind my back. Some of my sympathetic friends even wrote to me that they would [hurt themselves] if people were writing these kinds of things about them.

There is a national movement, promoted by many different groups, for teens to become "upstanders" rather than bystanders. An upstander stands up to cyberbullies and does not watch silently when other people are harassed and belittled online. Being an upstander does not mean criticizing the cyberbully or escalating the situation. It just means taking some sort of action to help the target and possibly put an end to the situation.

If you can do so safely, you can respond directly to the cyberbully online. Posting that you do not agree with what is being said and offering support to the victim is often enough to get the cyberbullying to stop. If you are worried you will be cyberbullied if you post publicly, you can still take other steps to help. Messaging the victim privately, reporting the abuse to the website platform, or reporting the cyberbullying to your school are all ways that you can be an upstander.

FIGHTING CYBERBULLYING

Cyberbullying is a problem that many teens around the world face every day, but it does not have to be that way. The more that people are educated about cyberbullying, the more they can do to stop it. It's everyone's responsibility to help the victims of cyberbullying and convince cyberbullies to stop their behavior. As people learn new methods of combatting cyberbullying, schools and communities are becoming stronger, healthier, and happier.

Glossary

adolescent A young person roughly between the ages of ten and nineteen.

aggression Hostile or violent actions.

anonymous Something said or written by someone whose identity is not known.

belittle To mock or put down.

blackmail To threaten to reveal something damaging to another person unless they do something.

bullying Intentional, repeated harassment that takes place in person. Bullying can be verbal, physical, or a combination of the two.

bully-victims People who both bully others and are themselves the victims of bullying.

bystander Someone who witnesses an event or occurrence but does not participate.

causation A relationship or connection between two variables in which one variable causes the other.

constructively In a positive way.

correlation A relationship or connection between two variables. Correlation is often confused with causation, but correlation does not factor in the cause of something.

cyberbullying Intentional, repeated harassment that takes place using digital platforms, including social media, multiplayer video games, and text messages.

epidemic A major, widespread outbreak of a disease or social problem.

explicit Fully shown, often used to refer to nude images.

harassment Behavior that threatens, pressures, or demeans a person or a group of people.

impersonation Pretending to be someone else.

Instant Messenger An early internet chat client.

intentional On purpose; not by accident.

moderation The process of keeping online communication appropriate by deleting offensive posts and comments.

retaliate To strike back at someone who wronged you.

throwaway account An online account that is used to anonymously post something.

traumatic Distressing, disturbing and shocking. People who experience traumatic events can have difficulty coping and can face long-lasting effects if they do not find positive ways to move forward.

unflattering Making someone look bad.

Further Information

BOOKS

Brown, Tracy. *Cyberbullying*. Helpline: Teen Issues and Answers. New York: Rosen Publishing Group, 2013.

Mapua, Jeff. *Coping with Cyberbullying*. Coping. New York: Rosen Publishing Group, 2017.

Scherer, Lauri S. *Cyberbullying*. Introducing Issues with Opposing Viewpoints. Farmington Hills, MI: Greenhaven Press, 2015.

WEBSITES

Cyberbullying

https://www.pacer.org/bullying/resources/cyberbullying

PACER's National Bullying Prevention Center provides information about cyberbullying, including a number of videos exploring the topic.

Cyberbullying FAQ for Teens

https://www.ncpc.org/resources/cyberbullying/
cyberbullying-faq-for-teens

The National Crime Prevention Council answers common questions about cyberbullying, such as how cyberbullying takes place, how to keep yourself safe online, and where you can find additional resources.

What Teens Can Do

https://www.prevnet.ca/bullying/cyber-bullying/teens

Canada's Promoting Relationships and Eliminating Violence Network talks about what teens can do to stop cyberbullying. The site also links to more resources.

VIDEOS

Cyberbullying, Bystanders, and the Role of the Upstander

https://onlinesense.org/cyber-bullying-bystanders-teens

Demi Lovato talks about her experience being cyberbullied and how important it is to stand up for other people.

5 Steps to Talking about Bullying

https://au.reachout.com/articles/5-steps-to-talking-about-bullying

Learn how to talk about being bullied or cyberbullied and get help.

Rethink Before You Type

https://www.youtube.com/watch?v=YkzwHuf6C2U

Teen Trisha Prabhu gives a talk on the dangers of cyberbullying and how the software she developed can help by giving people time to reconsider hurtful comments before they are posted.

Bibliography

ABC News. "Parents: Cyberbullying Led to Teen's Suicide." November 19, 2007. https://abcnews.go.com/GMA/story?id=3882520.

Anderson, Monica. "A Majority of Teens Have Experienced Some Form of Cyberbullying." Pew Research Center: Internet and Techology, September 27, 2018. http://www.pewinternet.org/2018/09/27/a-majority-of-teens-have-experienced-some-form-of-cyberbullying.

Athanasiou, Kalliope, Eirini Melegkovits, Elisabeth K. Andrie, Charalampos Magoulas, Chara K. Tzavara, Clive Richardson, Donald Greydanus, Maria Tsolia, and Artemis K. Tsitsika. "Cross-national Aspects of Cyberbullying Victimization Among 14–17-year-old Adolescents across Seven European Countries." *BMC Public Health* 18 (July 2018): 800–815.

Barnes, Jenna. "I Would Just Pounce: Cyberbully Reveals Identity, Why She Targeted Strangers." KSDK.com, April 17, 2018. https://www.ksdk.com/article/news/local/i-would-just-pounce-cyberbully-reveals-identity-why-she-targeted-strangers/63-540686450.

BBC News. "Amanda Todd Case: Accused Dutch Man Jailed for Cyberbullying." March 16, 2017. https://www.bbc. com/news/world-us-canada-39295474.

Berry, Keith. *Bullied: Tales of Torment, Identity, and Youth.* Abingdon, UK: Routledge, 2016.

CBC News. "Aydin Coban Sentenced in Dutch Court to 10 Years for Online Fraud, Blackmail." March 16, 2017. https://www.cbc.ca/news/canada/british-columbia/ aydin-coban-sentenced-netherlands-online-fraud-blackmail-1.4027359.

Cyberbullying Research Center. "Cyberbullying Facts." Accessed on January 1, 2019. https://cyberbullying. org/facts.

Cybersmile Foundation. "Lucie's Cyberbullying Story." August 24, 2017. https://www.cybersmile.org/blog/lucies-cyberbullying-story.

Ditch the Label. *The Annual Bullying Survey 2017.* July 2017. https://www.ditchthelabel.org/wp-content/ uploads/2017/07/The-Annual-Bullying-Survey-2017-1.pdf.

Enough Is Enough. "Cyberbullying Statistics." Accessed on January 1, 2019. https://enough.org/stats_cyberbullying.

Gordon, Sherri. "10 Facts About Cyberbullying Every Educator Should Know." *Verywell Family*, August 31, 2018. https://www.verywellfamily.com/facts-about-cyberbullying-for-educators-460708.

Low, Sabina, and Dorothy L. Espelage. "Differentiating Cyber Bullying Perpetration from Non-physical Bullying: Commonalities Across Race, Individual, and Family Predictors." *Psychology of Violence* 3 (January 2013): 39–52.

Madigan, Sheri, Anh Ly, Christina L. Rash, Joris Van Ouytsel, and Jeff R. Temple. "Prevalence of Multiple Forms of Sexting Behavior Among Youth: A Systematic Review and Meta-analysis." *JAMA Pediatrics* 174, no. 4 (April 2018): 327–335.

Media Smarts. "Cyberbullying and the Law." Accessed on January 18, 2019. http://mediasmarts.ca/digital-media-literacy/digital-issues/cyberbulling/cyberbullying-law.

Modecki, Kathryn L., Bonnie L. Barber, and Lynette Vernon. "Mapping Developmental Precursors of Cyber-aggression: Trajectories of Risk Predict Perpetration and Victimization." *Journal of Youth and Adolescence* 42, no. 5 (May 2013): 651–661.

Nixon, Charisse L. "Current Perspectives: The Impact of Bullying on Adolescent Health." *Adolescent Health, Medicine, and Therapeutics* 5 (August 1, 2014): 143–158.

Oprah.com. "Why One Father Is Struggling to Forgive Himself After His Bullied Son's Suicide." Accessed on January 1, 2019. https://www.oprah.com/own-where-are-they-now/john-halligan-12-years-after-his-sons-suicide-video.

WBUR. "Bullying; From Both Sides: Former Perpetrators and Former Victim Reflect on Past." March 20, 2018. https://www.wbur.org/hereandnow/2018/03/20/bullying-cyberbully-victim.

Index

About the Author

Derek Miller is an author and educator from Salisbury, Maryland. He has written numerous books for middle- and high-school students, including *Helping Yourself, Helping Others: Dealing with Opioid Misuse.* In his free time, Miller likes to read and travel with his wife.